This book belongs to:

____

The Pretty Little Wallflower

For My Daughter

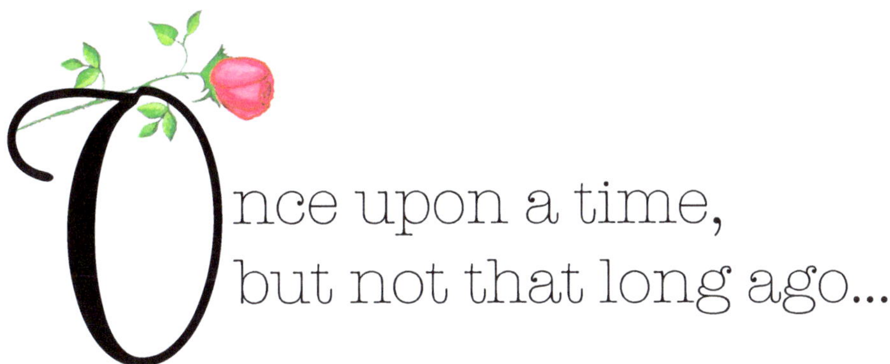

nce upon a time,
but not that long ago...

There lived a delicate little flower, a pink rose.

Her home was a warm, sunlit greenhouse that thrived in the middle of a bustling city.

She had big dreams and wanted to make her mark on the world.

HOTEL
THE URB

ARDEN

She got her start in the very back row
of the nursery, behind the taller flower
varieties like the Lillies, the Zinnias, and
her long-stemmed cousins.

She was smaller than the rest of the
flowers but she was no less beautiful.
In fact, her petals were closed tight but
they were the perfect shade of a girl's
favorite color.

PETALS
OPEN
111

When the flowers grew up and left the nursery, they moved into fresh flower markets and neighborhood florists.

There they were selected for bouquets and attended parties and other special occasions with their friends.

Sometimes, they were even chosen for the simple reason of making a room feel brighter.

But day after day, this sweet little
rose went unnoticed by all of the flowers around her. They just grew taller,
casting a shadow and taking her much
needed sunlight.

They also soaked up nearly every drop
of the daily water as their roots were
thick and seemed to stretch out in all
directions.

She was fighting
just to hang on.

She leaned on the wall when she
felt tired and stayed strong despite
her circumstances.

Then, one day, while cleaning the greenhouse and carefully weeding the flower beds, a nice gardener discovered the little flower all alone, in the very back.

She said "Hey little one, what are you doing back here? I'm sorry I didn't see you sooner."

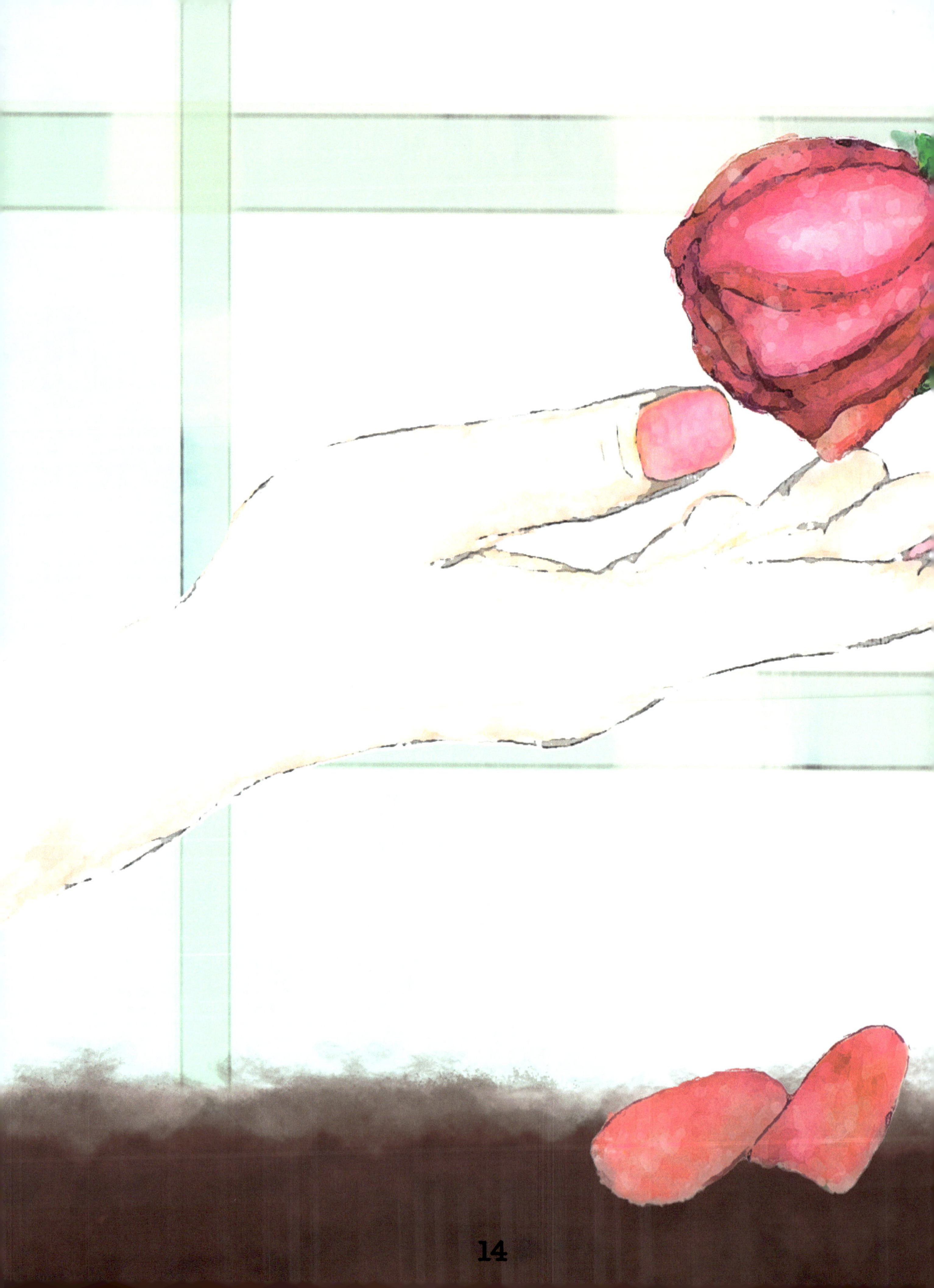

Then the gardener carefully
removed the precious flower
from the giant planter box
that she shared with the
other flowers and placed
her in a pot of her very own.

She gave her fresh potting soil and a
long drink of cool water.

She planted the tiny roots and stem
deep into the soil, making sure that
she felt secure.

Then she brought the little rose into
the center of the room so she could get
the most light and the best care.

This made the little flower very happy but she also felt a bit uneasy. She had never been the center of attention before. She felt as if the other flowers were staring at her and wondered what they would think.

But with a chance to thrive, she did just that. Her petals started opening up and revealing her complexity. Her stem straightened and this was giving her confidence. The once tender, green thorns were also becoming thicker to provide a protective shield.

And now, her fragrant petals filled the air with sweetness.

The gardener made time to visit with her every day and complimented her progress.

She kept away the weeds that tried to creep in and make her feel uncomfort-able.

She watched her blossom and became more and more proud of how strong the little flower had become.

At last, the delicate little wallflower was standing tall, on her own. Her petals were a beautiful and vibrant pink and they were fully open.

She turned her face into the sun and no longer worried what the other flowers thought of her.

And she would **never** have to lean

on the wall again.

About the Author:

Laura Tucker is a photographer, writer, illustrator and mother to a beautiful wallflower.

See more at
www.lauraktucker.com

Join our Facebook group here: